The 24-Hour Productivity Hack

Ali Ahmad

2023

The 24-Hour Productivity Hack

2023

Ali Ahmad

Illustrator: Abdullah Saleh

Erbil — KRG

CONTENTS

Introduction

The Agenda

* Make the most of the next 24 hours.

* learn a skill in 24 hours.

* 24 hours is enough for you.

* Everyone has 24 hours in a day, but how we use those hours is up to us.

* Don't let time slip away in your 24 hour session.

* A day in your life is the most important. — Now is important.

"Don't waste your time in anger, regrets, worries, and grudges. Life is too short to be unhappy."

— Roy T. Bennett

Reasons for Writing This Book

Although there are many reasons why an author might write a time-management book, my reason was something of an existential one. You see, **we only have 24 hours in a day**. To be frank, when we wake up, we are never quite sure if this is our last day or not. There is no way of knowing if this is the end for us or if we will still live to see tomorrow. Death is everywhere.

Many authors write time-management books for reasons other than death. — But for me, death was the driving force. because in reality, we only have today. — We either die or we stay alive for tomorrow.

We are really tricking ourselves and lying to ourselves when we try to manage weeks, months, and even years. The reality is that we only have today. That means, the moment we wake up at any given time of the day, this is our starting day. This day is the most important because we only have it once.

Therefore, the time between waking up and going to bed is very important because **a day is a life**. You must manage this time in the best possible way for your overall health and the health of others.

Always keep in mind that this day might be your last day. So don't be lazy, and don't be so quick that you might break something …

In summary

* Remember that death is always near, and you only have today. You cannot change yesterday, and you might not see tomorrow.
* Remember that this time window is important because this is all you have left for today. You might even have less left. But always be sure that this is all you have.
* Each day is a life. This day, this moment, is our life. There is no tomorrow. There is no yesterday. Let's do the best we can now, today. — And leave the rest to God.

"Time is an illusion."

— Albert Einstein

Why Is Time Management Important?

In today's fast-paced world, **everything is moving at an accelerated pace**. Consequently, even unimportant topics are gaining prominence. Therefore, it is crucial and wise to effectively manage our time and prioritize our attention towards meaningful topics and activities.

Of course, organizing and prioritizing your time doesn't have to be tedious and uninteresting. It should not feel like a robotic and obligatory task. It should come naturally and effortlessly. **Remember, the goal of time management is to support and empower you, not to restrict or burden you.**

The importance of time management is that it's not just time that is passing; it is also your own precious life that is passing away. Always remember this equation: **TIME EQUALS YOUR LIFE**. If you lose time, that means you are also losing life.

Dear reader, never underestimate the importance of time because it's your life. When you lose 5 hours, you are losing something that is impossible to bring back. Therefore, **time is the only true currency**. So, respect it.

Therefore, the time is yours. This is your life that we are talking about. No matter if your life is good or bad, important or unimportant, it is still a life that others and yourself depend on. **TIME EQUALS YOU**.

"You may delay, but time will not."

— Benjamin Franklin

Setting Goals for Time Improvement

When embarking on a journey of self-improvement, it is crucial to have a meaningful purpose. **This purpose should transcend mere temporary gains and aim for lofty heights**. The ultimate goal should be to enhance one's overall well-being, rather than being driven by material wealth, fame, or romantic pursuits. **Remain vigilant against the allure of superficial appearances.**

Setting goals for improving time management is a task that must be accomplished by analyzing what is the most important or what you believe to be the most significant aspect in your life. You should **carefully decide what stays with you in the next four years to come**. You are the chooser and the owner of your actions.

"The strongest of all warriors are these two

— Time and Patience."

— Leo Tolstoy, War and Peace

Identifying Time Wasters

THE LIST:

1. Procrastination: Delaying important tasks and putting them off for later.

2. Social media obsession: Spending excessive amounts of time mindlessly scrolling through social media platforms.

3. Multitasking madness: Attempting to juggle multiple tasks simultaneously, resulting in decreased efficiency.

4. Haphazard planning: Failing to establish a clear schedule or organize tasks effectively, leading to wasted time.

5. Meaningless meetings: Attending unproductive or unnecessary meetings that do not contribute to progress.

6. Prioritization pitfalls: Focusing on less

important tasks instead of prioritizing the crucial and urgent ones.

7. Distractions galore: Allowing interruptions, whether from phone notifications or unrelated conversations, to disrupt workflow.

8. response addiction: Constantly checking and responding to emails throughout the day, becoming a time-consuming habit.

9. Overthinking overload: Spending excessive time overanalyzing decisions or tasks, leading to indecision and inefficiency.

10. Superhero syndrome: Trying to handle everything alone without delegating tasks to others, resulting in overwhelm.

11. Unproductive downtime: Taking excessively long breaks or engaging in

unproductive activities that hinder productivity.

12. Time mismanagement: Ineffectively allocating time or underestimating the time required for tasks, causing delays.

Time-wasters are everywhere! Of course, we are not only talking about people, but also certain activities and hobbies that make us waste even more precious time.

It is true that we can list numerous time-wasting activities … However, the most impactful aspect of this discussion is the realization of how much time one is wasting in their own domain of life. **You must analyze your own time-wasters**.

For example, ask yourself this question —
**Today, what have I done that I hated
and regretted?** … This counts as a time-
waster. Most of the harmful activities that
we engage in waste a massive amount of
time. Therefore, one must cut these harmful
activities out of their life.

The most important point that people fail to
actualize is that what you do not prioritize
becomes a time-waster in itself. If you
cannot manage your day, that day will ruin
you. Therefore, it's always good to manage
your day before you start.

"Time takes it all, whether you want it to or

not."

— Stephen King,

Analyzing Daily Routines and Habits

There are 24 hours for everyone. It is not about the 24 hours … The numbers … It is about how you are willing to use them. And use them efficiently. You have to own them. You must love them. This is your life.

… By acknowledging your own faults and bad habits, you can begin to change and even diminish them to the point of forgetting them forever. This is why identifying and selecting bad habits are crucial.

[IMPORTANT NOTE]

Every bad habit was once just a < one-time trick> Never underestimate the energy and power of a bad habit. It will drag you down. It will slowly consume you. One attempt leads to many, and many leads to **THE COUNTLESS.**

Therefore, it is important to refrain from trying anything harmful or addictive right from the start. Nowadays, there are countless drugs and digital drugs that you haven't even experienced or know the names of. However, always remember that this is for the better, because if you try any of these, you will undoubtedly become hooked. Do not deceive yourself.

[CLARIFICATIONS]

It is indeed possible to quit bad habits and completely forget about them. However, it is even better to avoid trying them altogether. Now, I implore you, dear reader: Do not attempt them, so that you won't have to struggle with quitting them. Stay calm.

"Time present and time past

Are both perhaps present in time future

And time future contained in time past."

— T.S. Eliot

Conclusion

Hopefully, you will learn how to manage your overall time in a day and use the topics that have been discussed in this book for your overall productivity and drive.

Time management is an essential skill for anyone who wants to live a productive and fulfilling life. By identifying your time-wasters and bad habits, you can begin to make changes that will free up more time for the things that matter most to you. It is also important to set goals and priorities for yourself, so that you can focus your time and energy on the things that will help you achieve your desired outcomes. Remember, time is precious, so use it wisely.

"Your time keeps flying away into vanity while you dine with your distractions."

— Sunday Adelaja

The 24-Hour Productivity Hack

Introduction

What we're trying to do here is make the day reach its **full potential**. — We want to achieve **maximum productivity and a healthy mindset**.

As you may have noticed, if you set your goals too broadly and think that you can achieve them in a month or a year, you may find them to be unreachable. This is because you are setting yourself up for a slow and lazy approach. After all, **if you know that something can be done in a day, why would you wait a month or a year** to do it? …

The premise of this book is simple: **we want to achieve greater things in a short**

period of time. However, **we do not want to be impatient or reckless**. We want to be true to ourselves and do the job right, today.

"You can find something truly important in an ordinary minute."
— Mitch Albom

The Deadline

Imagine that you have **only 24 hours left** to live. What would you do with your time? …

If this scenario were true, you would go to your loved ones and forgive those who have wronged you. You would also work harder than ever before, knowing that this is your last moment. — Every breath and every drop of sweat would matter.

Live today as if this were you last. And indeed it is your last day. — Today is never the same as yesterday. Also tomorrow will not be the same as today. Everyday is unique and matters. — Put the days on top of each other like stacks of gold.

GO!

YOUR DEADLINE IS IN 24 HOURS!!!

"We are all migrants through time."

— Mohsin Hamid,

How Much Sleep Do You Get?

In this section, we will help you improve your sleep schedule. You should aim to get enough sleep so that you wake up feeling refreshed and energized, not groggy and tired.

There is a lot of debate about how much sleep people need, when they should go to bed, and what time they should wake up. — However, the ideal and healthy way to approach this topic is to find your own personal <sleep schedule> that works best for you. — This means finding a time to go to bed and wake up that allows you to get enough sleep without feeling groggy or tired throughout the day. It also means finding a routine that helps you wind down before bed and wake up refreshed in the morning.

Ask yourself and check your sleeping patterns. — Ask yourself: Does my sleeping pattern help me achieve a healthier mental and physical health, and does it also help me achieve my personal and communal goals? … If the answer to all of these is no, then you need to reevaluate your sleeping schedule and patterns.

Your sleep must be in line with your goals and your overall health. — If it is not, then it is time to change it to a healthier one. It is always possible to change for the better if you try.

If you think you are sleeping way too early or way too late, try to gradually adjust your sleep schedule by going to bed a little earlier or later each day until you reach your desired bedtime. Keep in mind that you may feel more tired than usual on some days, but try to resist the urge to sleep in. This will help you to adjust to your new sleep schedule more quickly.

Never underestimate sleeping. — Sleeping is just as important as waking up. Both are essential for our physical and mental health.

"Any time not spent on love is wasted."

— Torquato Tasso

The Fun Times

The fun times, the happy times, the non-working times: these are all titles given to a period of time in a day where an individual is free from work or anything related to work. It is a time to relax, to pursue hobbies, to spend time with loved ones, and to simply "enjoy life".

Of course, some people enjoy working and find it to be a fun and fulfilling activity. They may even include work as part of their leisure time. However, this is not the case for everyone. Different people have different preferences and what one person finds enjoyable, another person may not. It is important to respect these differences and to not judge others for their choices.

With that being said, it is important for an individual to identify their leisure times and fun times and decide what specific fun activity to spend their time on in a day. Because everyone has different ideas of what is fun.

Now as an individual, you might have an idea of what is fun for you. But most importantly, it is pivotal to find activities that are both fun and healthy. — As we know, many of the activities that are popular in our age are unhealthy and can lead to negative consequences. — Therefore, it is crucial to choose activities that are both enjoyable and beneficial to your physical and mental health.

For example, fun times in a day should include these criteria :

> **The activity should be healthy both physically and mentally.**

> **The activity should not harm others.**

> **The activity should be at least useful to achieve one of your small goals.**

***

[IMPORTANT REMINDERS]

Here are some examples of unhealthy fun activities and the reasons :

> **Spending too much time on social media :** Social media can be a great way to stay connected with friends and family, but it can also be addictive and time-consuming.

> **Over-Socialization** : Socializing is a fun activity, but too much of it can lead to self-absorption and isolation. It can also make other people feel disrespected and annoyed.

> **Undisciplined behavior** : is any behavior that distracts you from your goals and duties. — It can lead to an undisciplined life, which can ruin your life by making you lazy and forgetful.

"The memory of everything is very soon

overwhelmed in time."

— Marcus Aurelius

The Serious Hours

The serious hours are the productive hours of the day that you work to your full potential to achieve the best for yourself and the others around you. — That means not being distracted by any leisure activities or anything that is not related to your work.

When you are working during your productive hours, it is important to focus on your work and avoid distractions. — This means not checking your phone, not browsing the internet, and not engaging in any other activities that are not related to your work.

"CRY TODAY, LAUGH TOMORROW."

— Ali Ahmad

A Busy Day

In a busy day, always try to write down your goals for the day. This will help you stay organized and focused. You can write your goals on a small sheet of paper, in your daily journal, or in any other way that works for you. — There are many different ways to go about it, so find the one that fits you the best.

The best advice is to write down the most important <goals of the day>. — And they should be short and sharp. — Never try to write fancy. Write what you do not what you **will** not do.

"You never know when the truth will come home. You can't choose the time. The time chooses you."
— Rick Yancey, The Infinite Sea

Conclusion

The key to making the most of your day lies in finding a balance between productivity, leisure, and sleep. — Setting specific and achievable goals for the day can help you stay focused and organized. Remember to prioritize your physical and mental health by getting enough sleep and engaging in activities that are both enjoyable and beneficial. Avoid unhealthy distractions and stay committed to your work during your serious hours. — And finally, don't forget to laugh and have fun along the way. Life is too short to take everything too seriously. So, go ahead and make the most of each day, one goal at a time!

"Do not waste time for that is equal to wasting life."

— Sunday Adelaja

Fun Challenges

Introduction

To evolve into your fullest capacity, you must try some challenges in your life, and make it a little bit more spicy and noisy.

For example, The 24-hour challenge: This is a classic challenge where you set yourself a goal to complete something in 24 hours … — It could be anything from learning a new skill to completing a creative project.

Challenges are fun, but please be aware not to harm yourself in the process. And try your best to be healthy in every aspect of your life.

"You never know ahead of time what something's really going to be like."
— Katherine Paterson, Bridge to Terabithia

Learning a Skill in One Day

There are a lot of easy skills that you can learn a day. — especially if you are interested in the skill and you are willing to takeaway key points from the said skill.

For example, you can try to learn the basics of photography in one day … — With a skilled professional, they can teach you everything you need to know to get started. Of course, it's not about learning everything about photography overnight. It's about the journey of learning and developing your skills.

However, it can be a fun challenge to see if you can learn a skill in a day. There are many easy skills to choose from to get started.

"The work of memory collapses time."

— Walter Benjamin

Find Out Your Limits

A human is not human without limitations. — Everyone has their own set of limitations. The best thing to do is to know your limitations before they break you down!

There are many types of limitations in an individual's life. They can be physical, mental, emotional, or environmental. — But first of all, one must realize their limitations. One must not lie.

Forgetting your limitations can be harmful because you might become reckless and do things without thinking them through. This can lead to injuries, accidents, and other problems. It is very important to be aware of your limitations and to take them into account when making decisions.

It all depends on your past experiences to know your limitations in a field. For example, if you are tired after a hardcore photography session, then you can be assured that this is your maximum working limit. You should not overdo it, because **no productive work is more important than your own physical and mental health.**

Thus, it is very important for an individual to identify their secret limitations. If one knows more about their limitations, they will be more successful in life. **Self-awareness is key to success.**

"..time is always the price we pay for the
unlived life."
— André Aciman, Find Me

Conclusion

Learning new skills can be a rewarding and exciting experience. However, it's important to approach it with a realistic mindset and focus on the process rather than the outcome. — It's unrealistic to expect to master a new skill overnight, so it's important to be patient and persistent. Additionally, it's important to be aware of our limitations and respect them. — Pushing ourselves too hard can lead to burnout and frustration. Instead, we should focus on making gradual progress and celebrating our small wins. By taking this approach, we can enjoy the journey of learning and improvement without feeling overwhelmed or discouraged …

"If you waste a minute, you have wasted life and if you waste an hour, you have wasted life."
— Sunday Adelaja

Back-Matter

Dedication

Acknowledgement

About

Glossary of Terms

Dedication

Dedicated to those who wasted time, and

those who wish for a better life.

Dedicated to the Kurds.

Acknowledgement

* I am grateful to **Abdullah Saleh** for providing the overall design materials for this release.

* I am grateful to **Zachary Wood** for helping me come up with the perfect book title.

* I am eternally grateful to those who helped me complete this book. Without your help, I could not have done it.

About

Ali Ahmad

I am a Kurdish writer who strives to produce better content and information for the overall benefit of humanity, and to bring knowledge to others around the globe.

Contacts

Mail: ali.ahmad.krd@gmail
Youtube: Ali.Ahmad.H
Instagram: ali.ahmad.krd
Tiktok : ali.ahmad.h

Release Designer

Instagram : Fuji_xv

Whatsapp : +9647512308044

Works

<u>kurdish</u>

1. مرۆڤ له لووتكهدا؛ ههولێک بۆ باشترکردنی ژیان
2. چۆن قسه بکهین
3. ئهخلاق به سادهیی
4. وههمی سهرکهوتن
5. چهند سهرنجێک لهسهر ڕووخساریهت: ژیل دۆلۆز و فیلێکس گواتاری
6. چهند سهرنجێک لهسهر تهمهن
7. ئاشنابوون به زانستی ژیربیژی
8. ههشت یاسای جهنگهڵ

<u>English</u>

9. Mental Cornucopia

10. The 24-Hour Productivity Hack

***

Glossary of Terms

Procrastination: Deliberately delaying important tasks, leading to inefficiency and time wastage.

Social Media Obsession: Excessive and unproductive use of social media platforms, consuming valuable time.

Multitasking Madness: Attempting to handle multiple tasks simultaneously, often resulting in decreased effectiveness.

Haphazard Planning: Failure to create a structured schedule, causing time to be wasted on disorganized tasks.

Meaningless Meetings: Attending unproductive or unnecessary meetings that do not contribute to progress.

Prioritization Pitfalls: Focusing on less important tasks over critical and urgent ones, leading to wasted time.

Distractions Galore: Allowing interruptions, like phone notifications or unrelated conversations, to disrupt workflow.

Response Addiction: Constantly checking and responding to emails, consuming excessive time throughout the day.

Overthinking Overload: Spending excessive time overanalyzing decisions or tasks, resulting in inefficiency.

Superhero Syndrome: Attempting to manage everything alone without delegating tasks, leading to overwhelm.

Unproductive Downtime: Engaging in excessive breaks or unproductive activities that hinder overall productivity.

Time Mismanagement: Ineffectively

allocating time or underestimating the time required for tasks, causing delays.

Existential: Pertaining to existence, especially in a philosophical context that explores the nature of being and purpose.

Groggy: Feeling disoriented, drowsy, or sluggish, often after waking up or due to lack of sleep.

Reckless: Acting without proper consideration for potential risks or consequences.

Superficial: Concerned with only the surface or apparent aspects of something, lacking depth.

Self-Absorption: Excessive focus on oneself to the detriment of awareness of others or the outside world.